SMILE SCHOOL

Written by Julie Flynn

JULIE FLYNN
SMILE SCHOOL

ISBN: 978-1775331445

Book Design | Julie Flynn

Dedicated to the young readers who are taking the first steps in learning to care for their teeth.

Welcome to Smile School!

Today, we will learn how to keep our teeth strong and smiles bright!

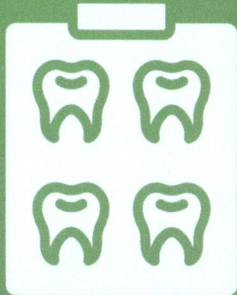

Smile School

Why Do We Need Teeth?

Teeth help us chew food, talk, and share big smiles with our friends!

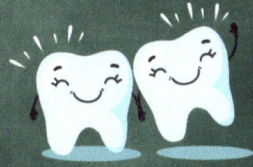

Fun Fact: Teeth are the hardest parts of our bodies!

Who Keeps Our Teeth Healthy?

- That's your job!
- Family helps; grown-ups remind us to brush our teeth.
- The dentist performs checks to ensure teeth stay healthy.

Teeth Care Team

You

Your Family

The Dentist

Meet The Brush Buddy

The toothbrush is your teeth's best friend; it's soft bristles help keep teeth clean!

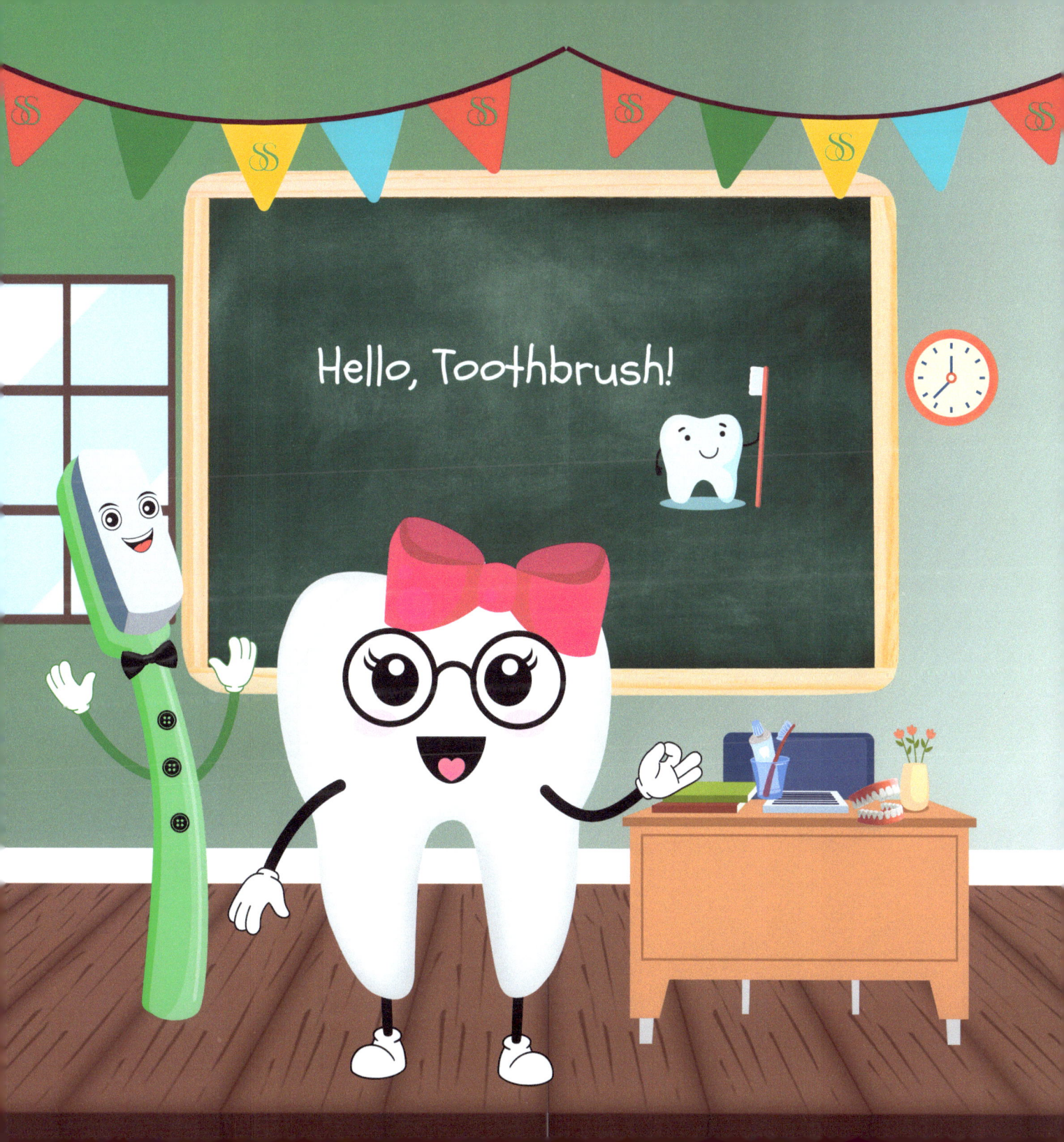

Hello, Toothbrush!

Toothpaste Powers

Toothpaste has foaming ingredients that protect and polish our teeth. Together, toothpaste and a toothbrush are the perfect pair for strong, healthy teeth!

Fun Fact: A pea-sized dab of toothpaste is all you need.

Sugar Bugs

Sugar bugs are tiny germs that stick to teeth, which can make teeth sad. Brushing every day keeps sugar bugs away and makes teeth happy!

Sugar Bugs Be Gone!

Before Brushing   During Brushing   After Brushing

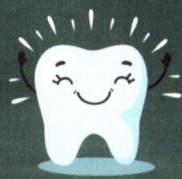

The Brushing Moves

Brush teeth in all directions, by moving the brush gently up and down, from side to side, and in circles all around. Make sure each side of the tooth gets a turn!

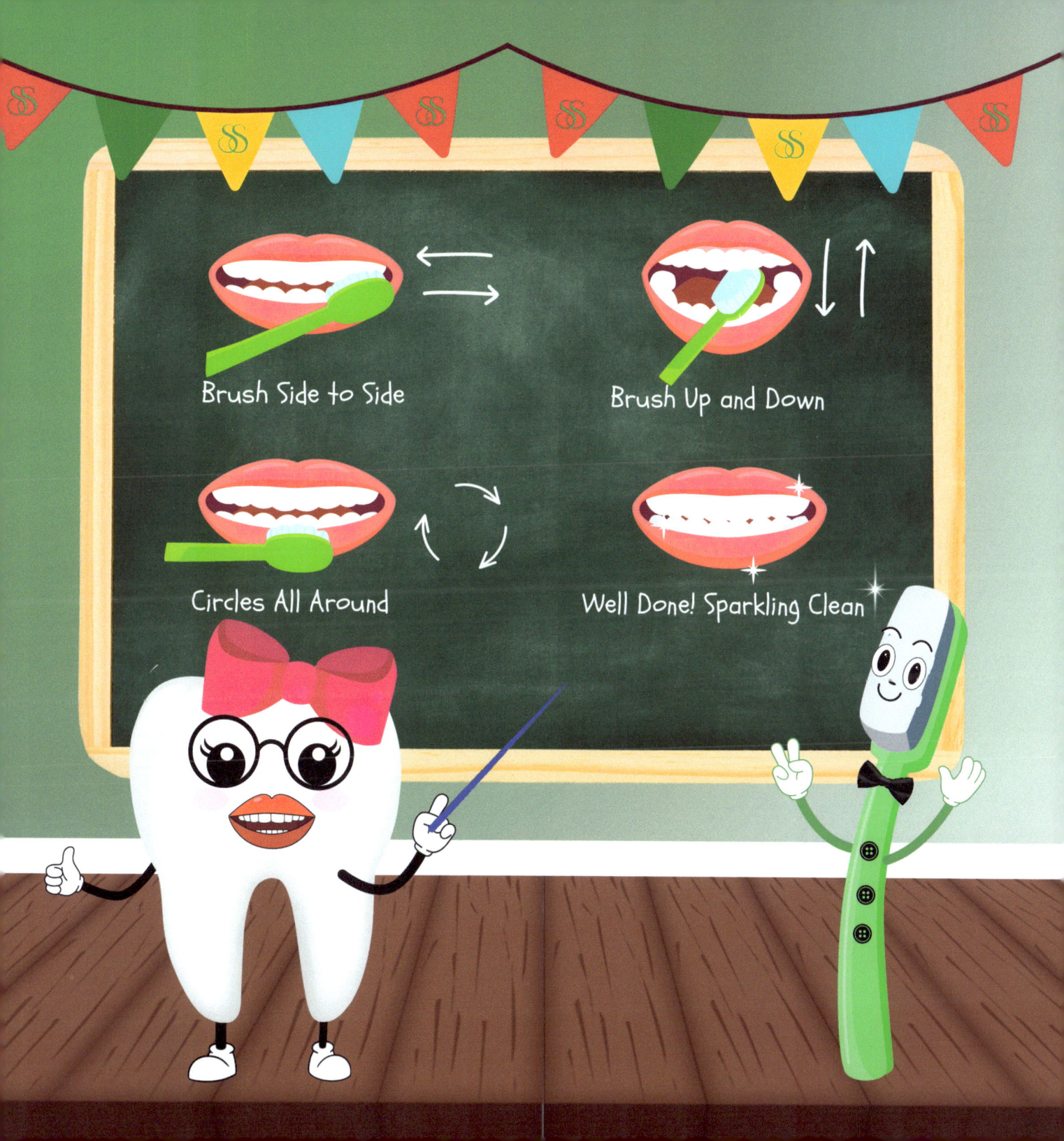

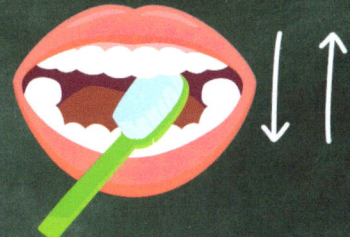

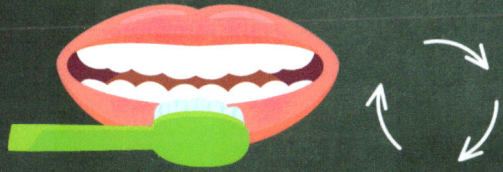

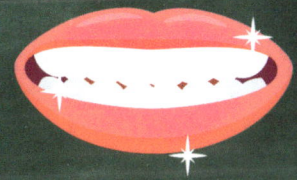

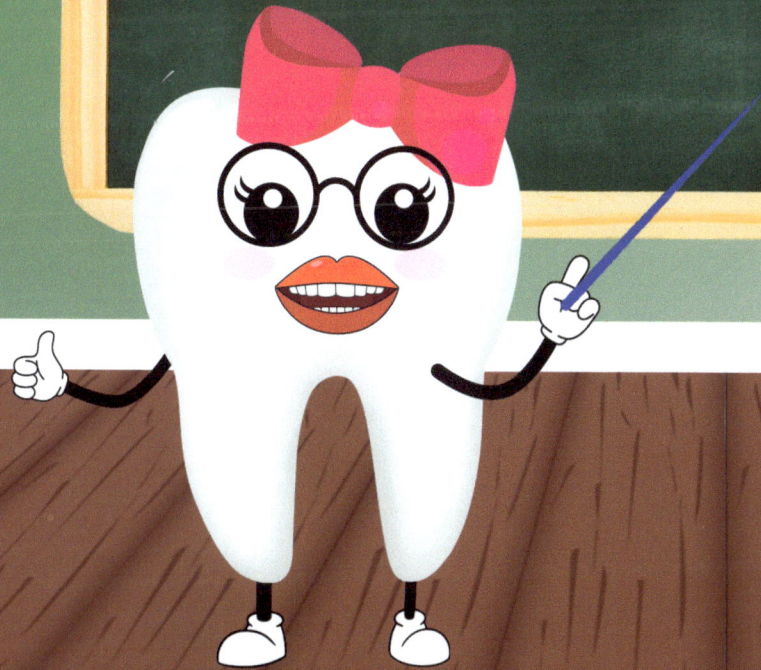

Brushing Adventure!

Set a timer for two minutes, and hum along to your favourite song while you clean every tooth!

Fun Fact: Two minutes of brushing well helps teeth stay clean and healthy!

2 mins

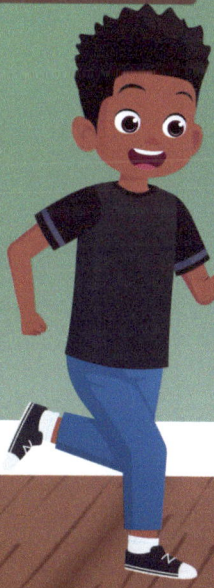

Happy Teeth Song!

Hold your toothbrush in your hand,
Squeeze out a dab of toothpaste, just a little strand.
Brush, brush gently, one, two, three,
Foamy bubbles you can see.

Brush side to side, up and down, all around,
No sugar bugs to be found.
Stay focused, you're nearly done,
Brushing is so much fun!

Now spit out the foamy bubbles,
All teeth are happy and clean, no troubles.
Shiny smiles are here to stay,
Twice a day, that's the way, hooray!

Tooth Brushing Station

Spit and Smile!

After brushing, spit out the foamy toothpaste into the sink; there is no need to rinse with water! The little amount of toothpaste left on your teeth will provide extra protection!

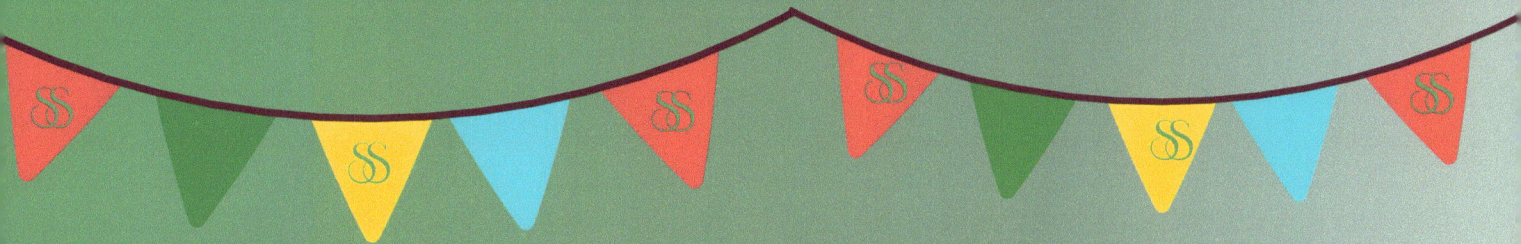

Celebration Time!

Wow! We have learned why we need teeth and how to keep them clean and healthy.

Remember to brush twice a day and to visit the dentist! Dentists are smile heroes; they check that our teeth are strong and stay happy!

Weekly Brushing Chart

Brush for 2 minutes day and night,
add a star on each tooth, and watch
your smile shine! ✦

	Week 1 ☀ 🌙	Week 2 ☀ 🌙	Week 3 ☀ 🌙	Week 4 ☀ 🌙
Monday	🦷 🦷	🦷 🦷	🦷 🦷	🦷 🦷
Tuesday	🦷 🦷	🦷 🦷	🦷 🦷	🦷 🦷
Wednesday	🦷 🦷	🦷 🦷	🦷 🦷	🦷 🦷
Thursday	🦷 🦷	🦷 🦷	🦷 🦷	🦷 🦷
Friday	🦷 🦷	🦷 🦷	🦷 🦷	🦷 🦷
Saturday	🦷 🦷	🦷 🦷	🦷 🦷	🦷 🦷
Sunday	🦷 🦷	🦷 🦷	🦷 🦷	🦷 🦷

Time to count!

Can you spot every tooth, toothbrush, toothpaste, smile, and timer?

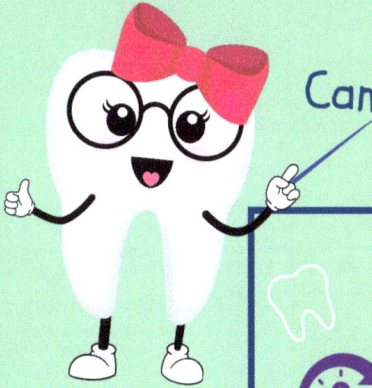

Tooth: __   Toothpaste: __   Toothbrush: __

Smile: __   Timer: __   Grand Total: __

www.ingramcontent.com/pod-product-compliance
Lightning Source LLC
Chambersburg PA
CBHW042110040426
42448CB00002B/208